This Book Belongs To

NOTE TO PARENTS

Welcome Little One, Learn to Write First Workbook will be fun and easy. Give your child a head start with our latest preschool learning book that teaches tracing and writing with fun lines, shapes and colors.

PRACTICE MAKES PERFECT
DEVELOP FINE MOTOR SKILL
LETTERS, NUMBERS AND SHAPES

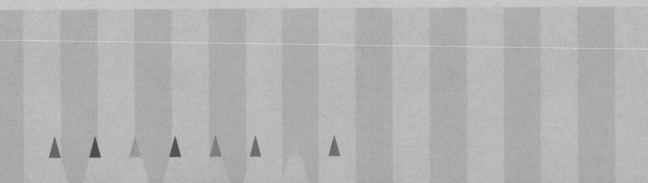

Trace each dotted line with a crayon.

Trace each dotted line with a crayon.

Trace each dotted line with a crayon.

Trace each dotted line with a crayon.

Trace each dotted line with a crayon.

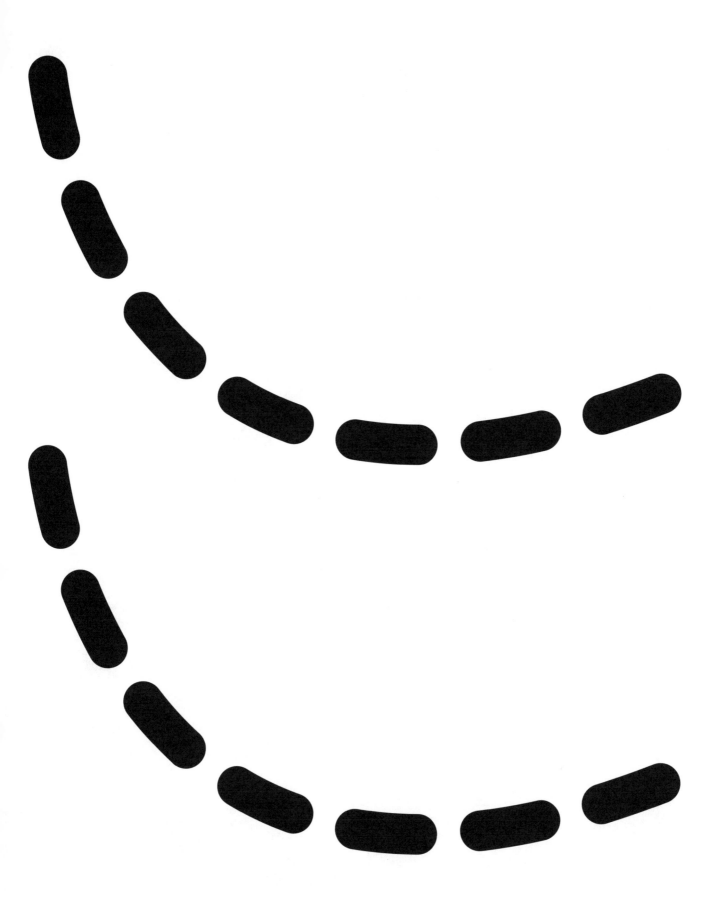

Trace each dotted line with a crayon.

Trace each line with a crayon.

Trace each line & dotted line with a crayon.

- -

_____

- -

_____

- -

_____

Trace each dotted line with a crayon.

Trace each dotted line with a crayon.

- -

- -

- -

- -

- -

Trace each dotted line with a crayon.

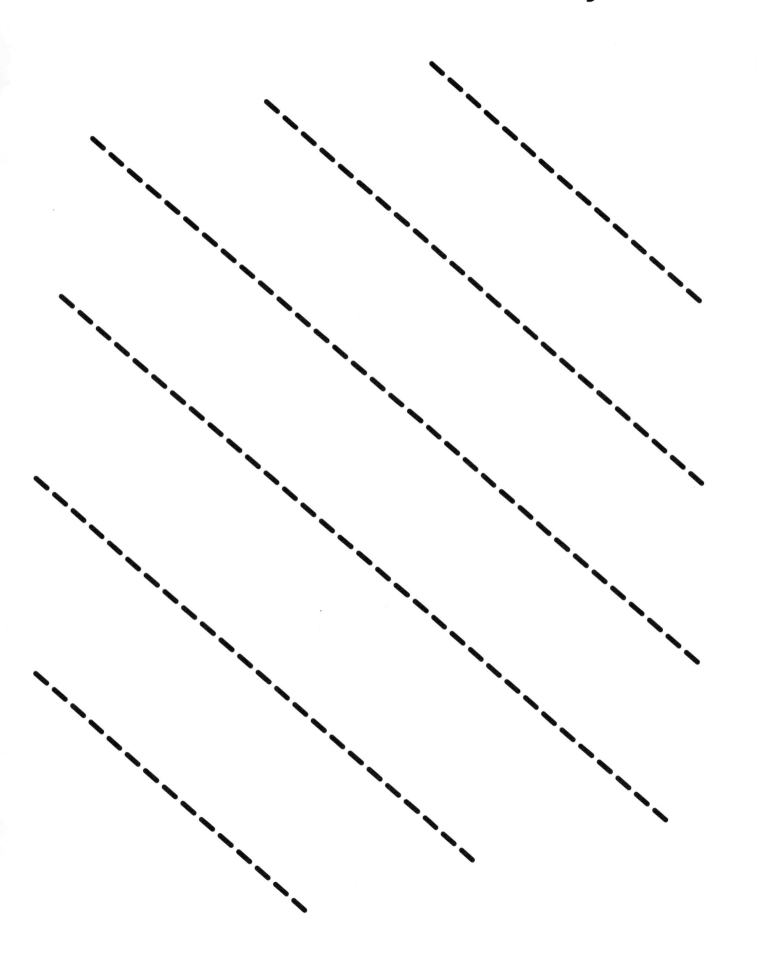

Trace each dotted line with a crayon.

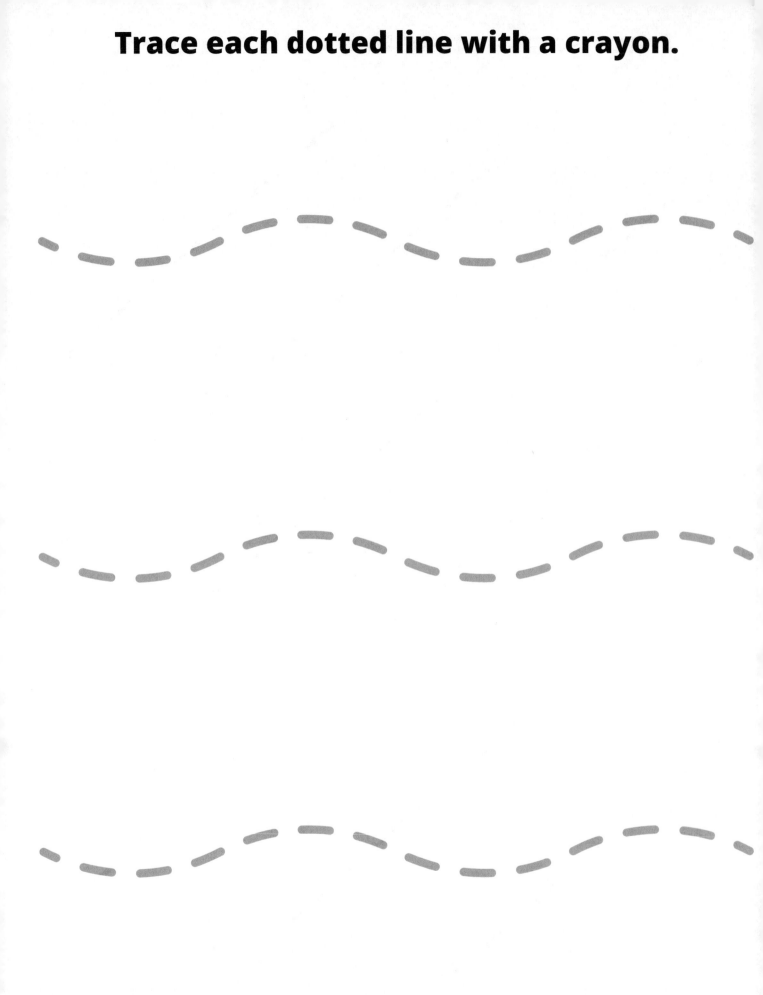

Trace each dotted line to each animal, lets name each animal.

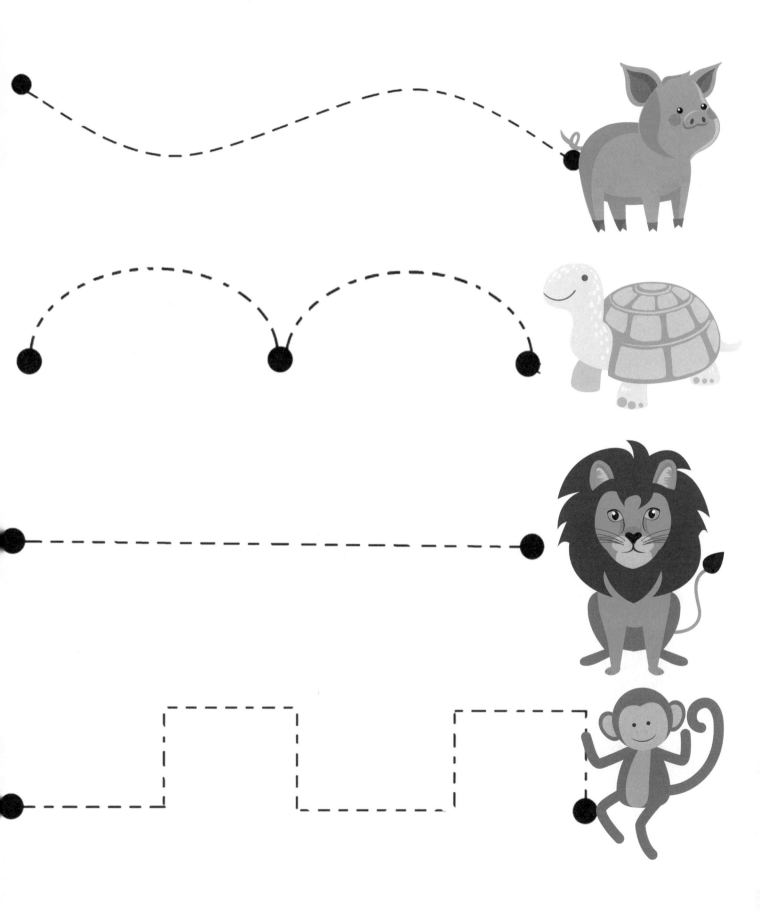

Trace each dotted line to each plane, lets trace and name each color.

Trace the lines to help the drivers make it to the finish line!

Trace the uppercase letter.

A for 🍎 Apple

Trace the lowercase letter.

a for ant

Trace the uppercase letter.

B for 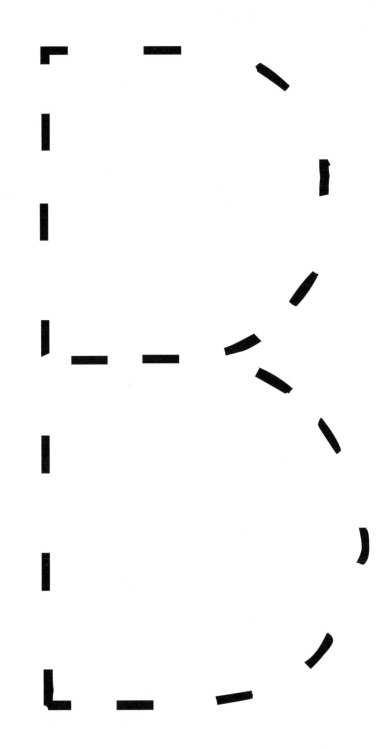 Bee

Trace the lowercase letter.

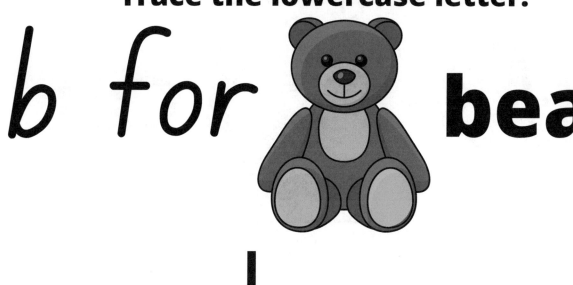

b for bear

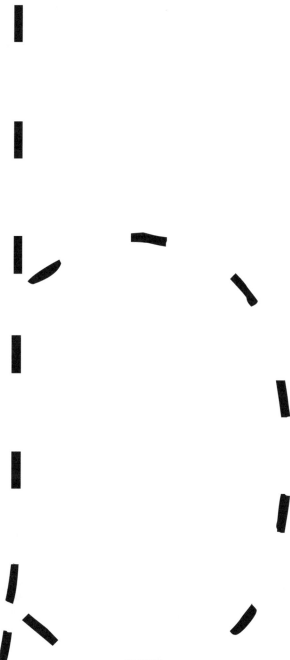

Trace the uppercase letter.

C for Cat

Trace the lowercase letter.

c for  cow

Trace the uppercase letter.

D for  **Duck**

Trace the lowercase letter.

d for 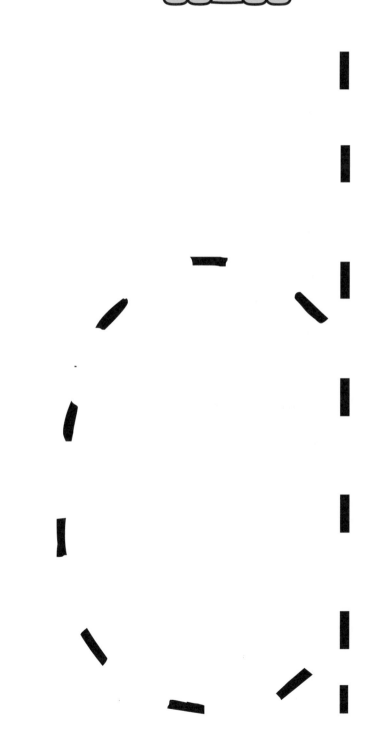 **dog**

E for  **Elephant**

Trace the lowercase letter.

e for 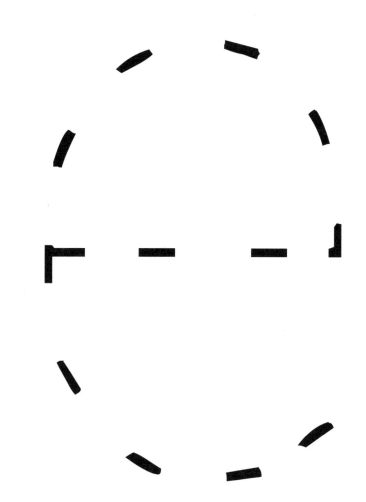 **eggs**

Trace the uppercase letter.

F for Fish

Trace the lowercase letter.

f for 🐸 fog

G for Goat

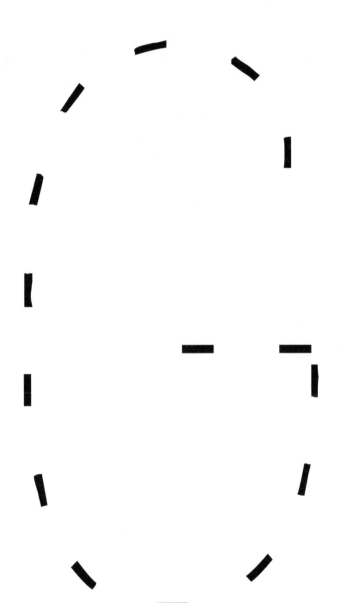

Trace the lowercase letter.

g for 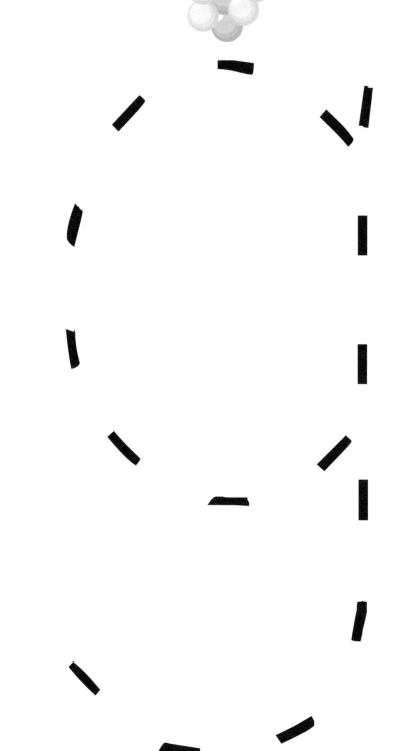 grapes

H for Horse

Trace the lowercase letter.

h for 🏠 **house**

I for Ice cream

Trace the lowercase letter.

i for igloo

I
I
I
I
I

Trace the uppercase letter.

J for  Juice

Trace the lowercase letter.

j for jump

Trace the uppercase letter.

K for  **Kite**

Trace the lowercase letter.

k for 🔑 **keys**

L for  **Lion**

Trace the lowercase letter.

l for 🪵 **log**

‌ ‌ ‌ ‌ ‌ ‌ ‌ ‌ ‌ I
‌ ‌ ‌ ‌ ‌ ‌ ‌ ‌ ‌ I
‌ ‌ ‌ ‌ ‌ ‌ ‌ ‌ ‌ I
‌ ‌ ‌ ‌ ‌ ‌ ‌ ‌ ‌ I
‌ ‌ ‌ ‌ ‌ ‌ ‌ ‌ ‌ I

Trace the uppercase letter.

M for Monkey

Trace the lowercase letter.

m for 🌙 **moon**

Trace the uppercase letter.

N for  **Nose**

Trace the lowercase letter.

n for  nest

Trace the uppercase letter.

O for 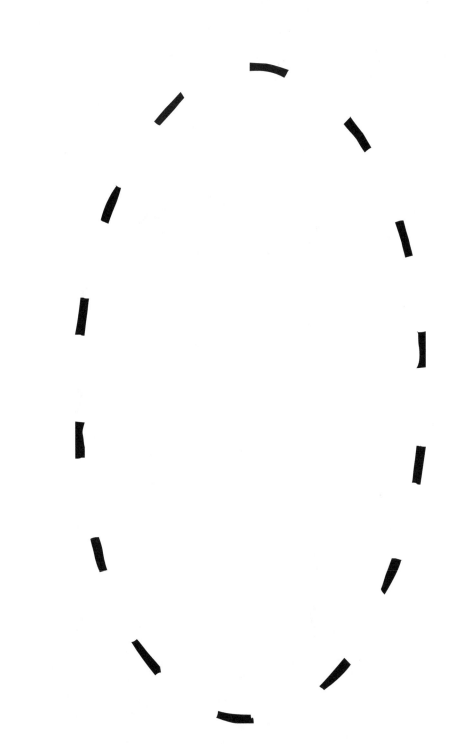 **Octopus**

Trace the lowercase letter.

o for orange

Trace the uppercase letter.

P for 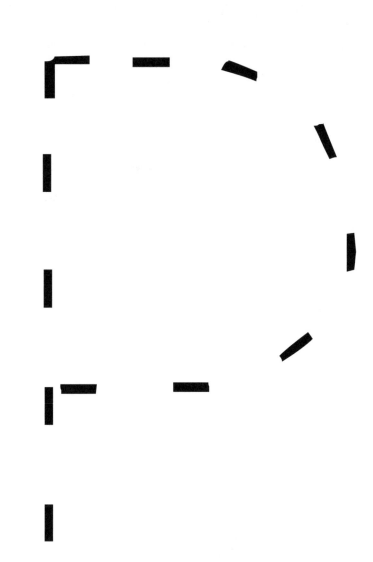 **Pig**

Trace the lowercase letter.

p for 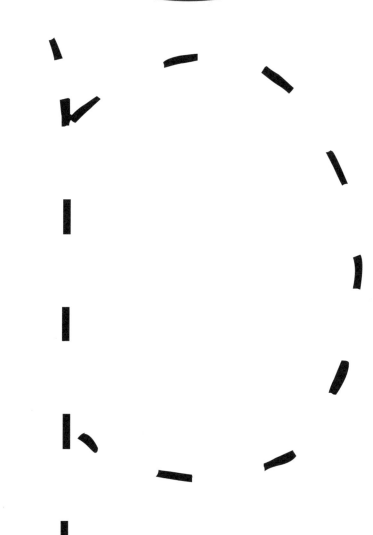 **plant**

Trace the uppercase letter.

Q for 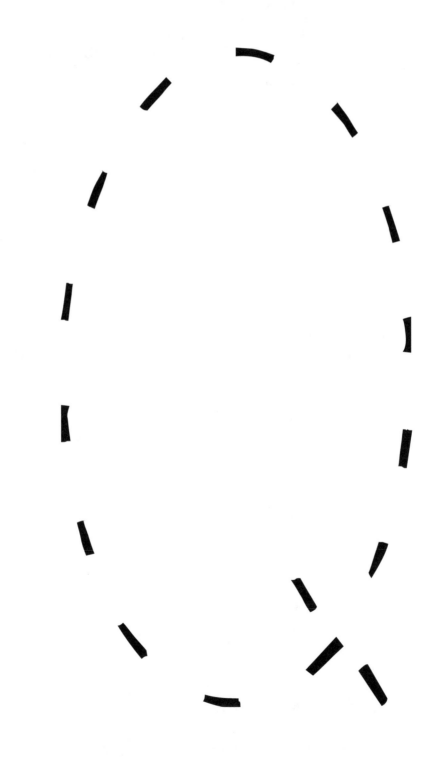 Queen

Trace the lowercase letter.

q for quarter

Trace the uppercase letter.

R for Rabbit

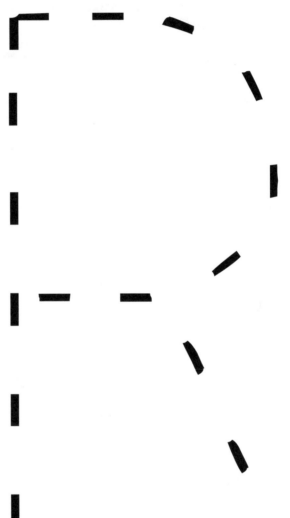

Trace the lowercase letter.

r for 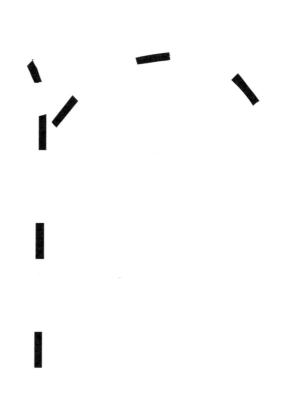 **robot**

Trace the uppercase letter.

S for Snake

Trace the lowercase letter.

s for 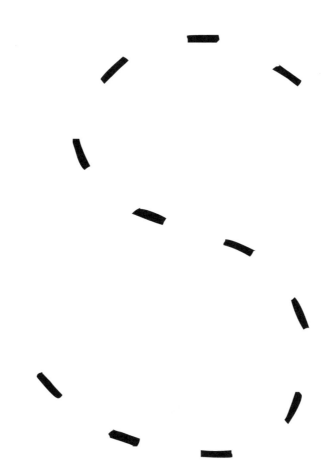 **sun**

T for Tiger

Trace the lowercase letter.

t for **toy**

‖

Trace the uppercase letter.

U for 🌂 Umbrella

Trace the lowercase letter.

u for 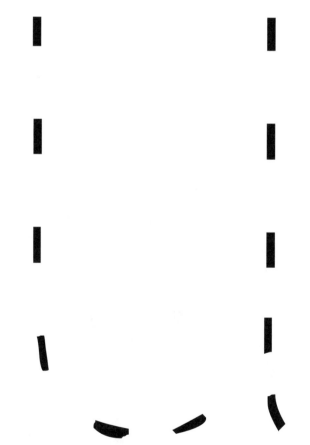 underwear

Trace the uppercase letter.

V for 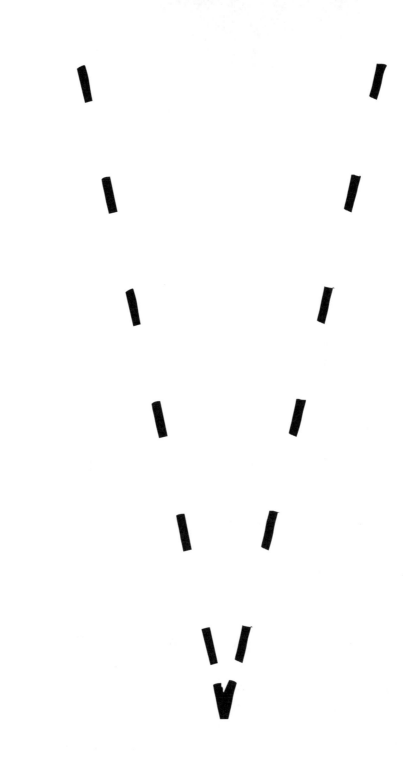 Van

Trace the lowercase letter.

v for  volcano

Trace the uppercase letter.

W for **Whale**

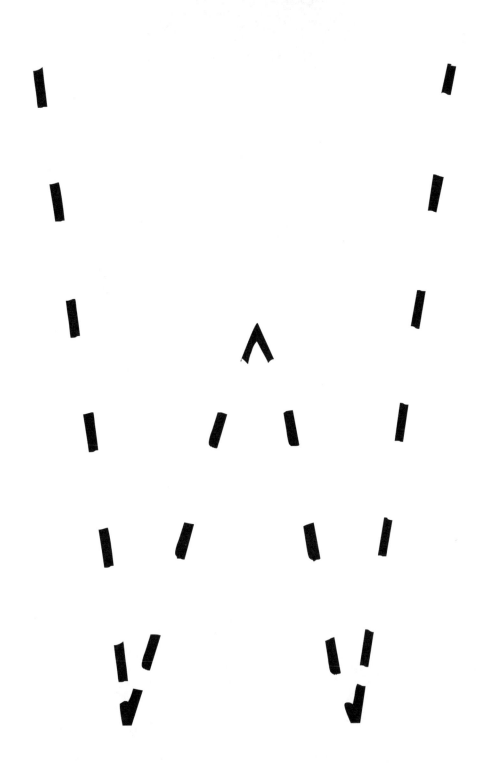

Trace the lowercase letter.

w for  **wagon**

Trace the uppercase letter.

X for  **X-ray**

Trace the lowercase letter.

x for 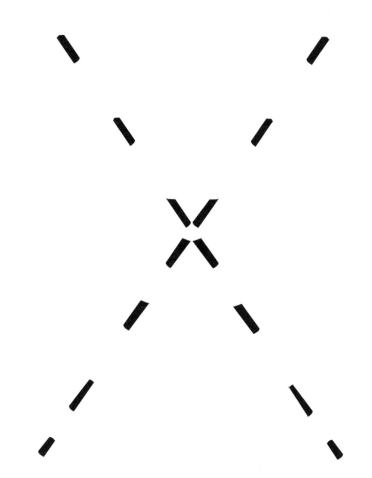 xylophone

Y for Yarn

\ /
\ /
\ /
Y
|
|
I

Trace the lowercase letter.

y for yak

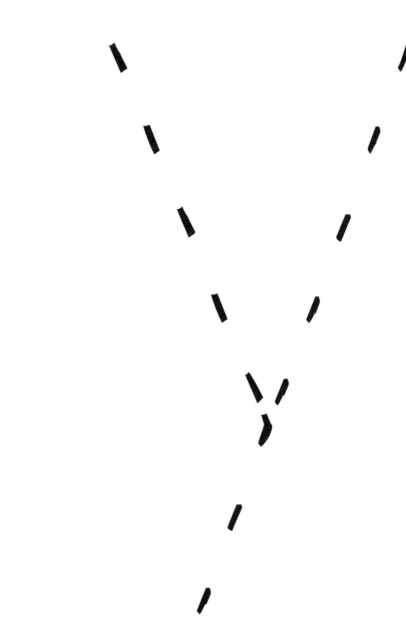

Z for Zebra

Trace the lowercase letter.

z for zipper

Trace each lowercase letter.

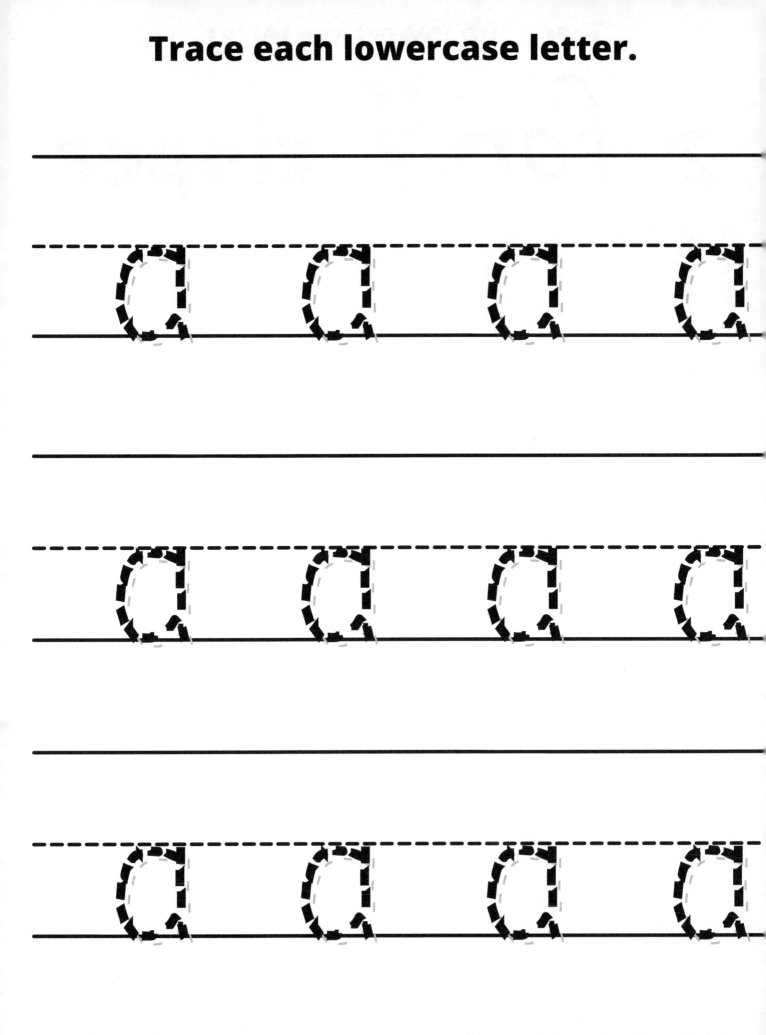

Trace each lowercase letter.

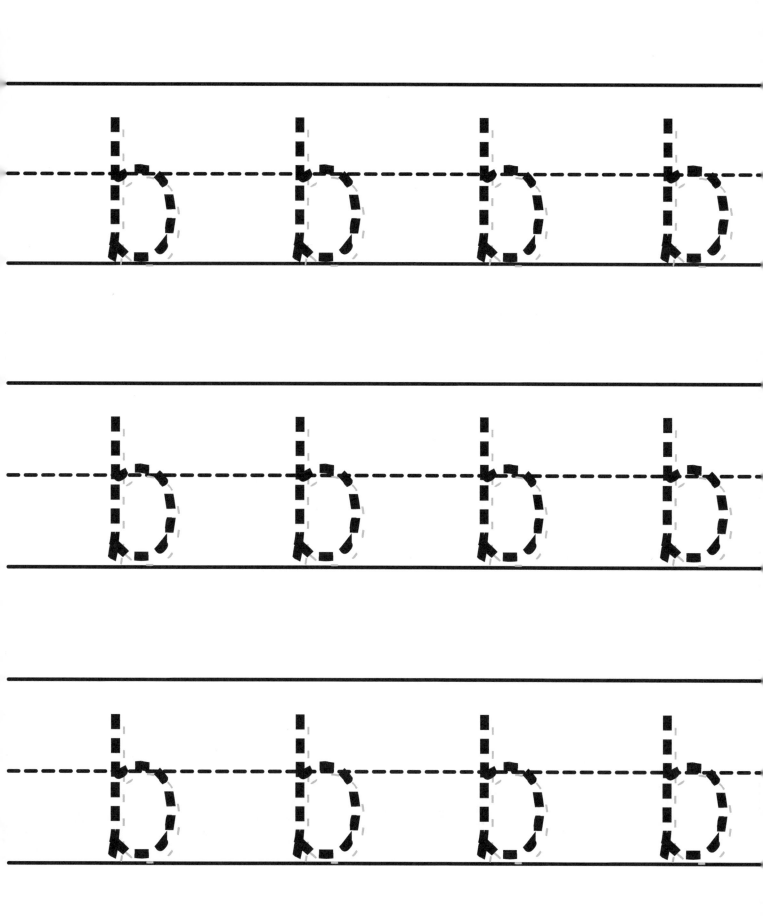

Trace each lowercase letter.

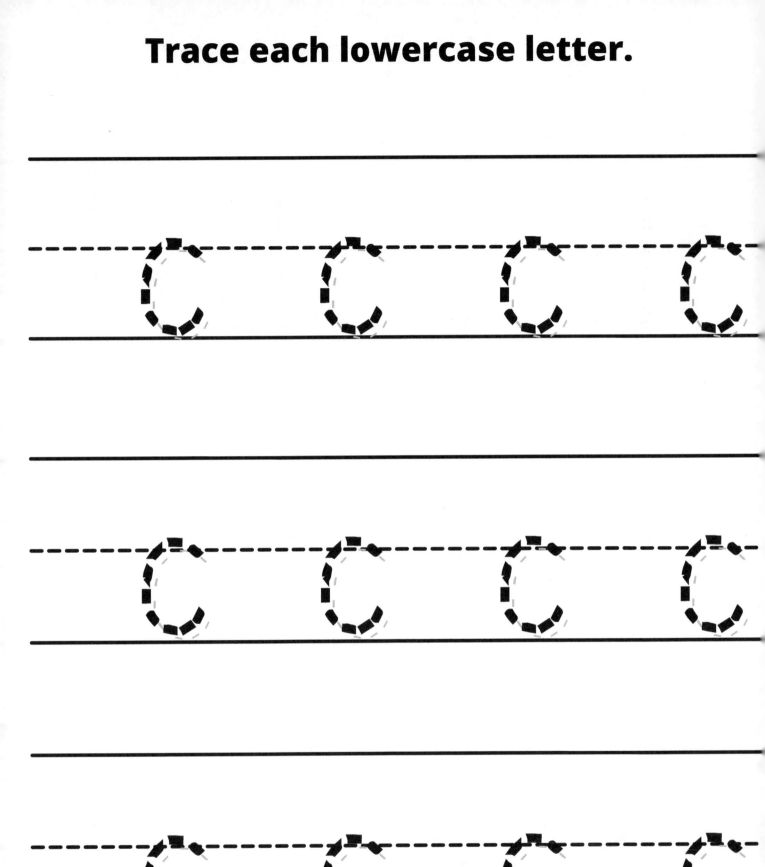

Trace each lowercase letter.

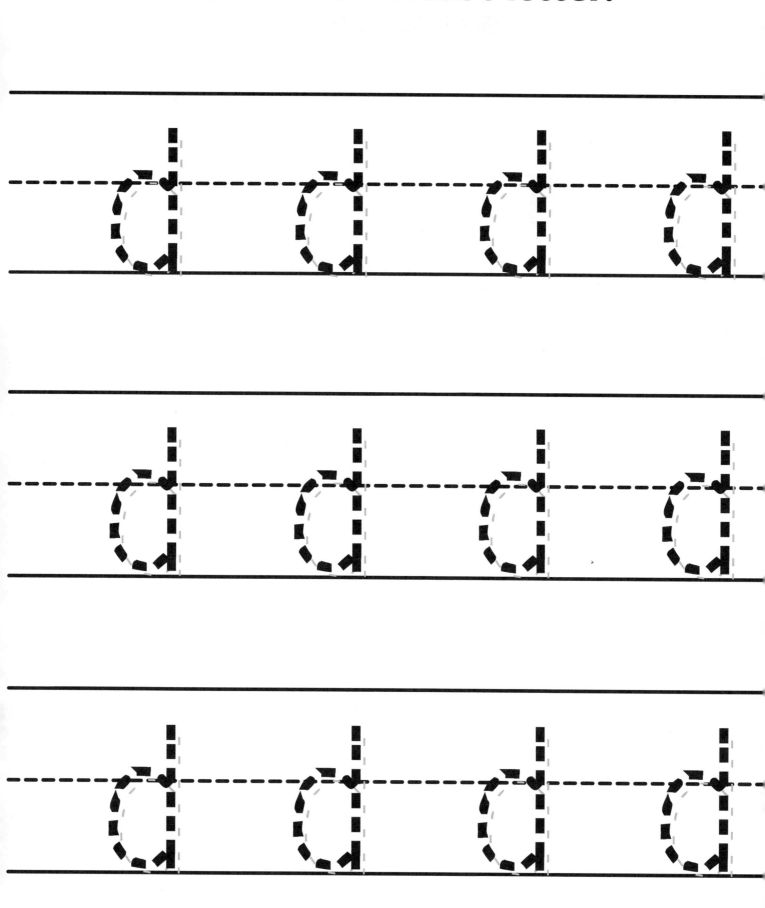

Trace each uppercase and lowercase letters.

Trace the words that begin with the letter a.

apple

actor

arrow

alligator

ant

Trace the word and the number.

Trace the word and the number.

Trace the word and the number.

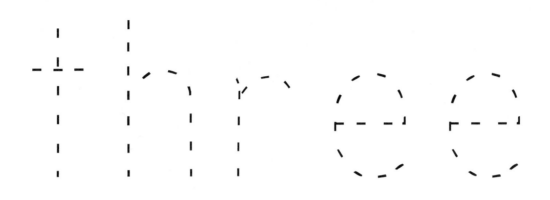

Trace the numbers 1, 2 & 3. Take your time

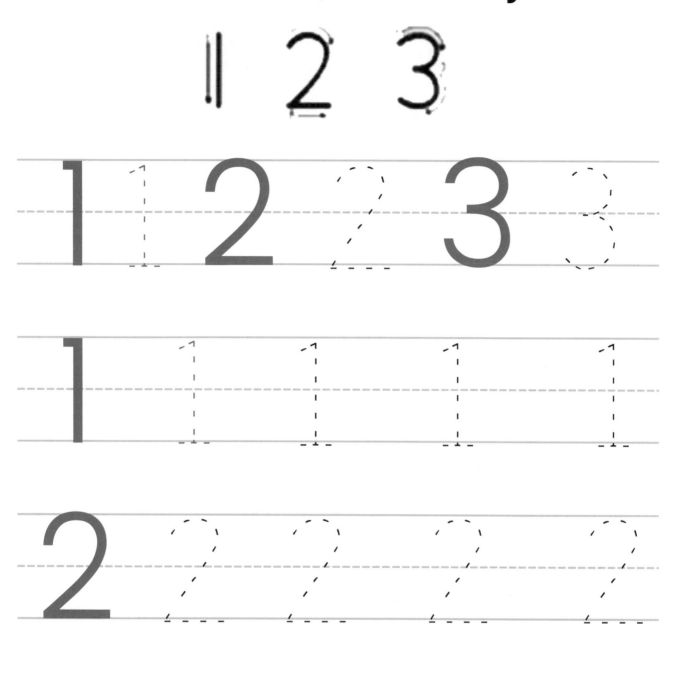

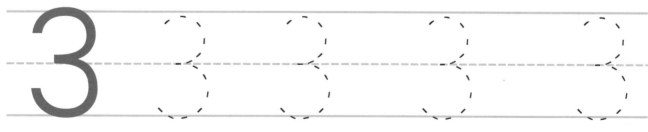

Trace the numbers, lets count items.

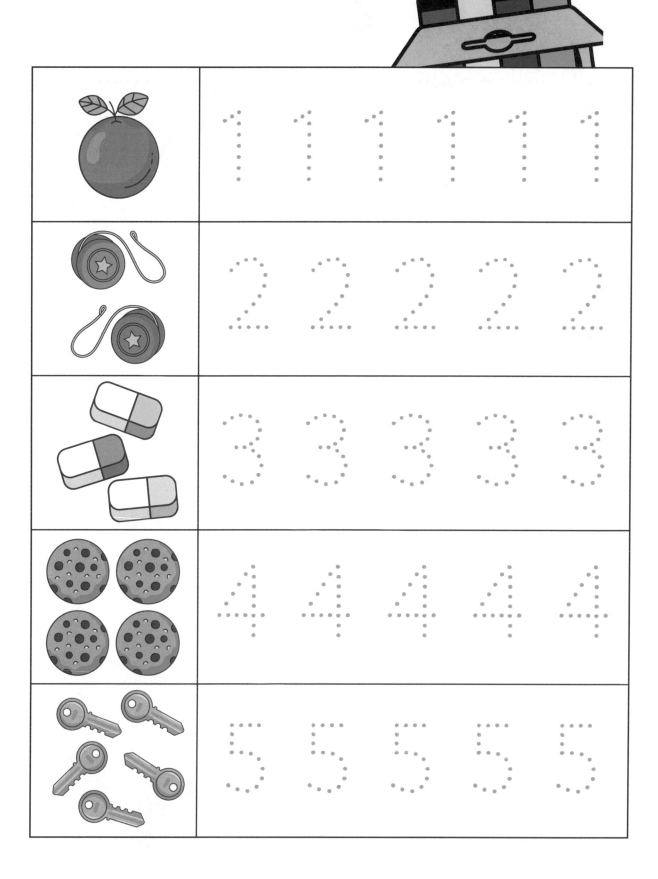

Trace the words and numbers below to practice the number five. Color the number.

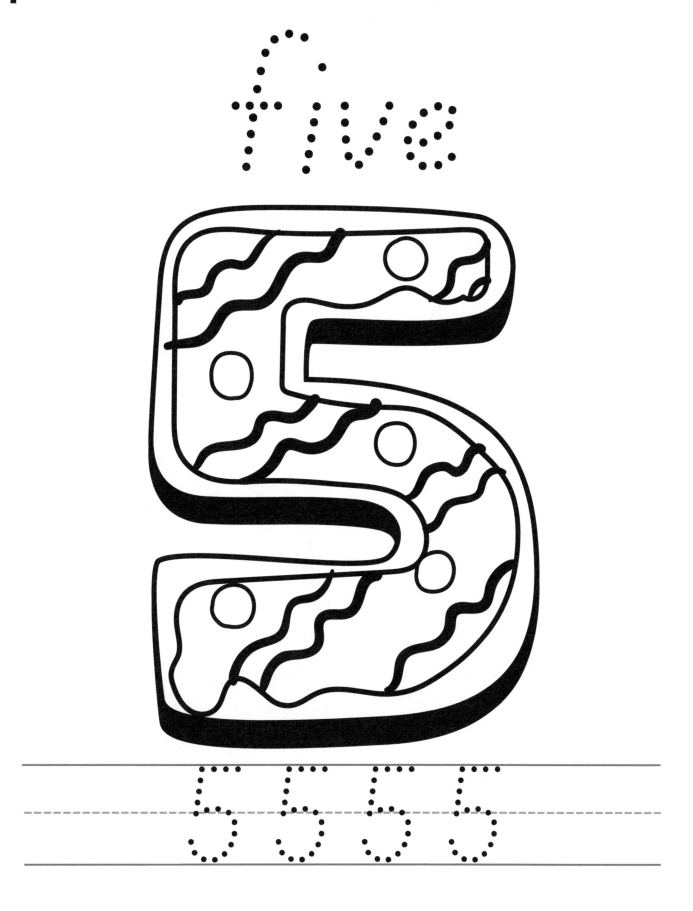

Trace the shape, lets name the shape.

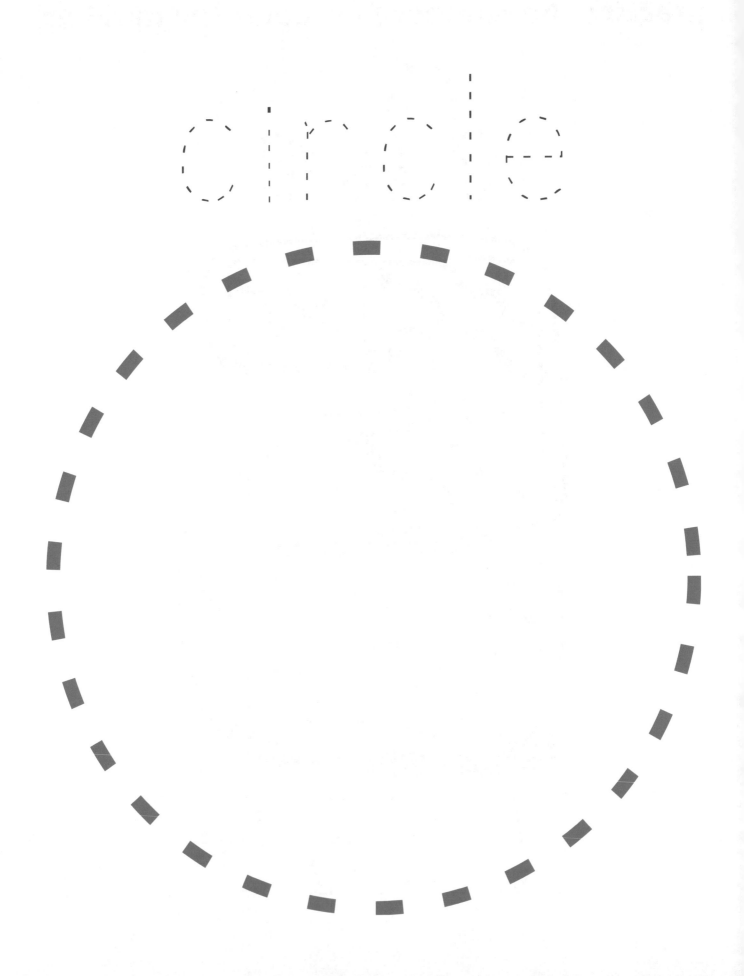

Trace the shape, lets name the shape.

Trace and color in the shapes below.

Trace each shape, lets name each shape.

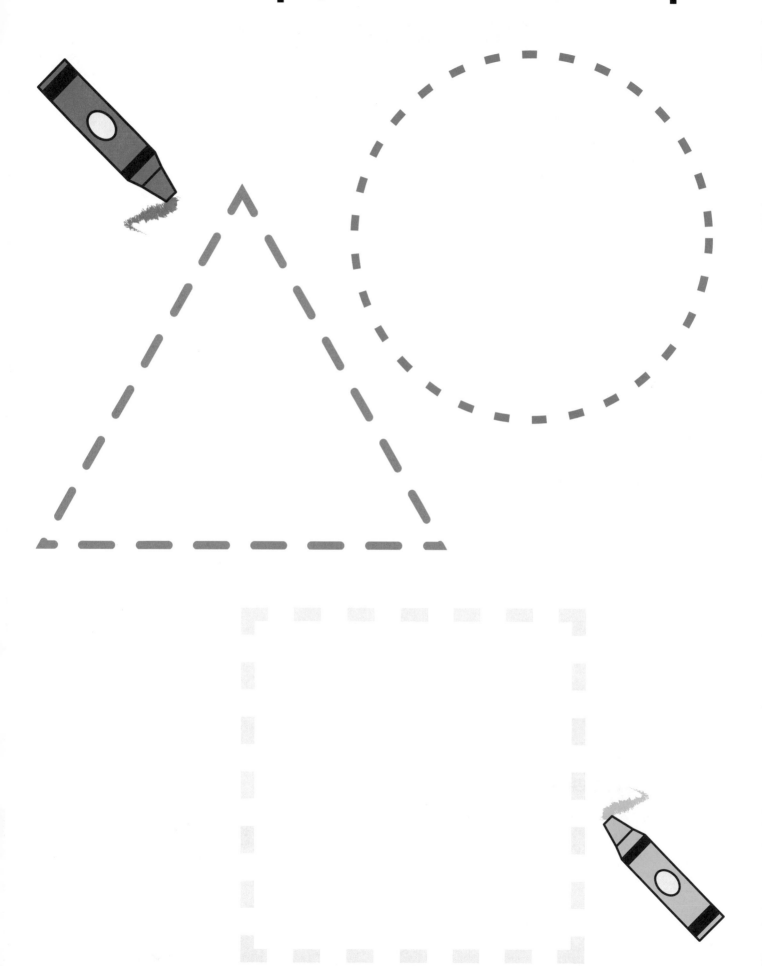

Trace each shape and letters remember to take your time.

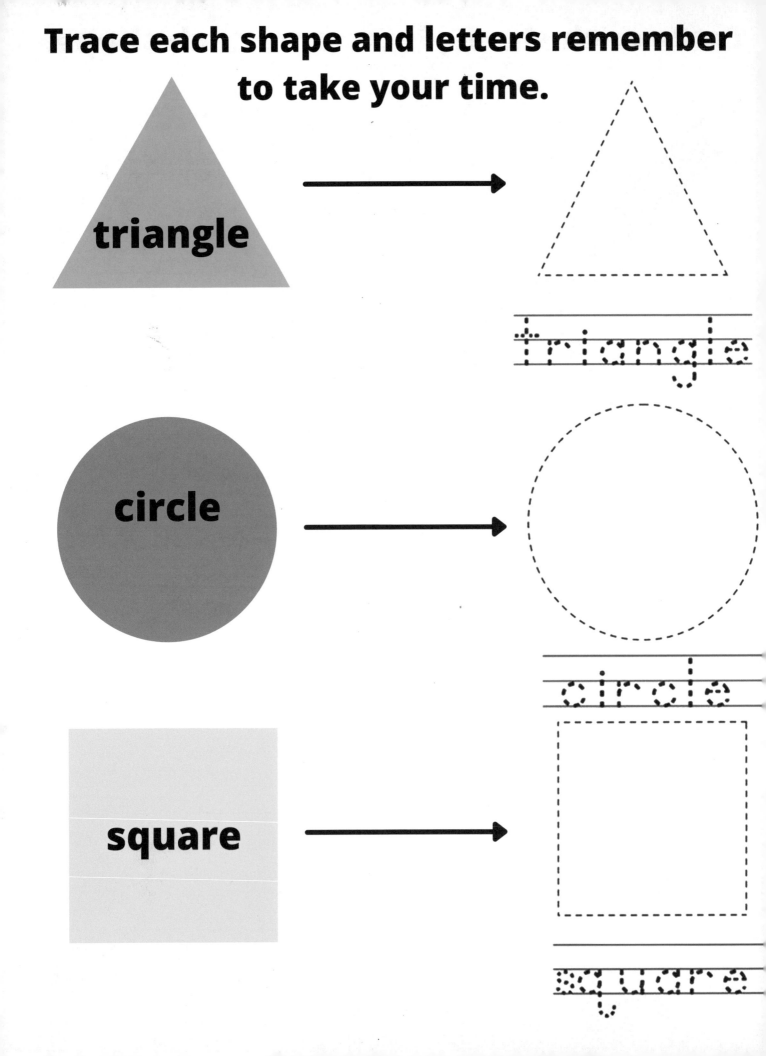

Trace each shape and letters remember to take your time.

rectangle

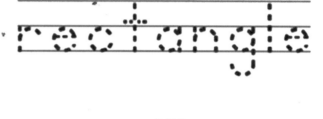

oval

diamond

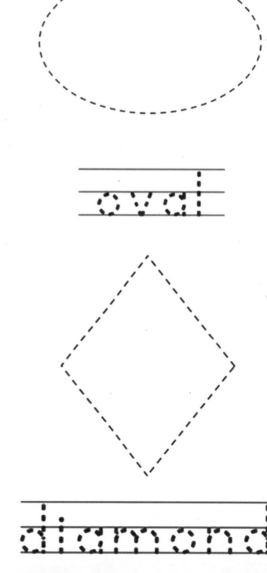

Trace the banana and the letters. Now lets color the banana.

Banana

Banana

Trace each shape, then color the picture. Can you name the shapes?

Truck

Trace each shape, then color the picture. Can you name the shapes?

Kite

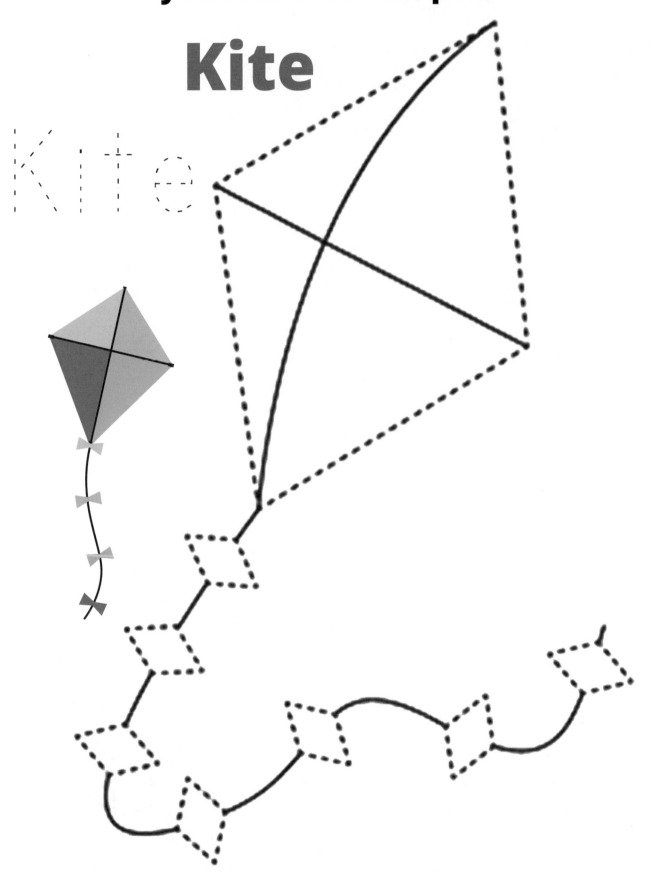

Trace the dinosaur and the letters. Now lets color the dinosaur.

Dinosaur

Dinosaur

Trace and color these fairy tale characters.

FAIRYTALES

Trace each number.

Trace each letter uppercase letters.

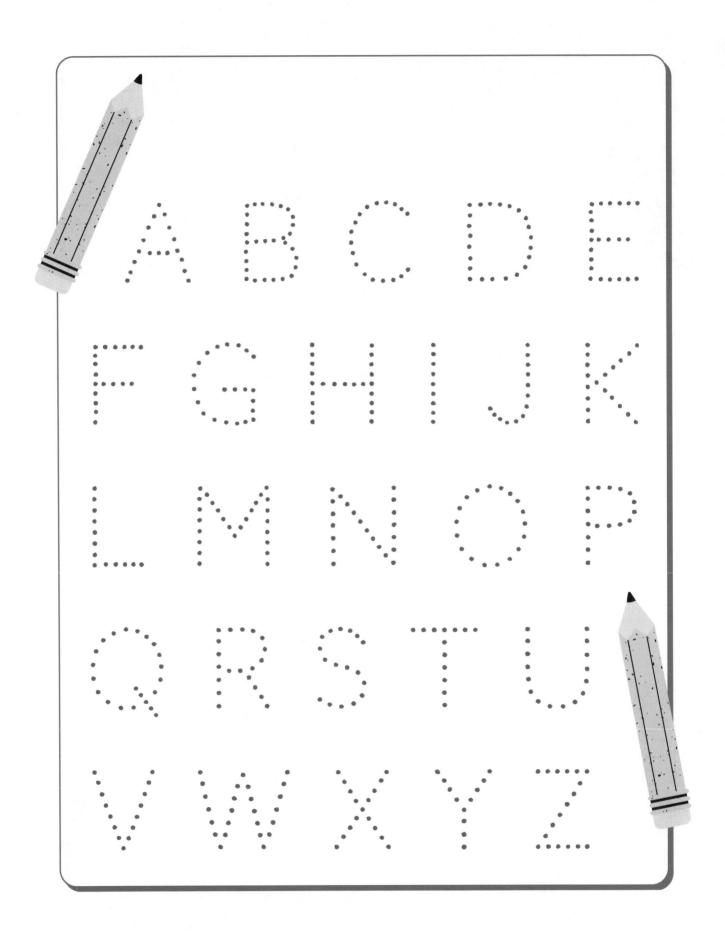

Write child name using dots and let your child trace their name.

Write child name using dots and let your child trace their name.

Practice tracing blank sheets.

Practice tracing blank sheets.

Practice tracing blank sheets.

Certificate of Completion

This certificate is persented to

_____

· ·

_____

for learning to write

Date _____

Made in the USA
Columbia, SC
14 April 2024

34028329R00057